Copyright © 2018 Dr Daniel Anders

All rights reserved.

ISBN: 978-0-9995677-2-2

DEDICATION

A special thanks and appreciation to my wife, Pamela, for her encouragement, insight and emotional support. To Stephanie Fuerte for her editorial skills and observations. To Margaret Corser for her illustrative talents. To the many golfers that have struggled with the mental aspect of the game, allowing this golfer the opportunity to share a means to overcome temporary handicaps. Enjoy!

CONTENTS

	Introduction	1
1	Why Peaceful Golf	4
2	Understanding the Subconscious Mind	6
3	Conscious Conflicts	13
4	Common Approach to Curing Golf Woes	15
5	Competition	18
6	Understanding and Overcoming the YIPS	22
7	Eliminating the YIPS	26
8	Peaceful Golf	29
9	How to Make Your Own Recording	34
10	What Should Be Contained in the Recording	37
11	Using Peaceful Golf Concepts with Every Day Life	40
12	Junior Golf	41
13	Scripts	43
14	Closing Comments	46

INTRODUCTION

Have you noticed the "improvement" trend in golf? It is hard not to be aware of the various types of opportunities to enhance your golf game. The club improvements are just as diverse as the types of golf balls to utilize. There is now a golf glove designed to provide yardage distance to the hole. There is head-wear with a device that identifies whether you are in the zone. Golf attire now allows sweat to be removed from the skin. And there is the forever forgiving putter. Even the golf cart has become a modified entertainment center. But there is one element of golf that has not changed due to gimmicks or modifications: it is how you "think" while playing golf.

There are many thoughts that go through the mind while playing golf, and for many, the mind is also very active during the moment of making the golf swing. The thinking of golf has not changed since the beginning of the creation of the game. Just read the many instructional books from the early years and you will find the same content as the current instructional books – minus modified terminology. The process of thinking can be broken down to a few steps, the first being a cognitive or mental awareness. From this awareness comes a subconscious response, which leads to the body reacting to the subconscious messaging. That is a simplistic explanation, but that is all that is needed to be aware of how the mind operates without going into biochemical and physiological changes. But here is the important part - *what is being thought at the moment of the golf swing is what is changeable.*

My approach to thinking and golf starts in the subconscious area of the mind. I have focused on this area because of my experience with working with the subconscious while helping clients manage personal and professional concerns. You see, I'm a licensed mental health professional and I have discovered that utilizing the subconscious part of the mind is the most efficient way to make long term changes and establish a proactive approach to help avoid unwanted thoughts – usually the negative thoughts...which is why it is an excellent tool to improve your golf game. I call the approach, Peaceful Golf – and the basis of the process is to remove the negative approach to playing golf.

This book will be divided into sections to explain how Peaceful Golf can be attained and a few popular areas of where it can be valuable. Although the subconscious explanation can be overly technical, my approach to explaining the subconscious mind will be presented in an easy-to-understand manner so that the process of Peaceful Golf can be readily understood and applied. I will also provide examples of the various areas of applicability, with a step-by-step explanation of how you can train your mind to not be so punishing while playing the wonderful game of golf. You will also learn of how folks weaken their golfing confidence by making the harmless sarcastic remarks and grunting negative inner-thoughts. It is amazing how just a few changes can shift your disposition of fright, fear, agitation, hesitation, aggression, and intolerance to a transition of playing golf peacefully, and with a fun enthusiasm. Shouldn't golf, for most folks, be a relaxation from life, and not a pressure from life? I think so – which is why Peaceful Golf is such an applicable program.

Why Peaceful Golf? Peaceful Golf was developed due to friends wanting help with the mental side of their game, and my personal desire to whip the YIPS. This book will explain how easy it is to eliminate first tee jitters, putt 2-footers without being nervous, comfortably chip over water without worry, be confident with your shots – especially with an audience or with a course marshal slowly rolling within your peripheral and mental view, and avoid having the negative thoughts overtake your mental game before you even tee off on the first hole.

In addition to this, for folks with the YIPS – I will explain how to control and eliminate the phenomenon that has driven many professionals out of the game, and a major reason why recreational golfers quit. If you don't know about the YIPS, a full explanation is provided.

So, get comfortable, read this book slowly and enjoy what is being explained and presented – your subconscious mind will appreciate it.

1 WHY PEACEFUL GOLF

In 1977, I found myself enjoying golf less as I fell victim to the YIPS. I went on an adventure to overcome the YIPS, and I exhausted almost every conceivable method available over the next 30 years. Some of the tactics that I used were almost comical: tensing every muscle right before striking the ball, closing my eyes as I putted, visualizing the ball going to the hole, changing grips, changing stances, and even using a rubber band around my wrist to snap when I felt the onset of the YIPS.

For those who may not know, the YIPS are a combination of muscle tension and spasmodic thinking right before hitting a golf ball. For me, it was a complete blackout at impact. I would literally have no vision of the ball making contact with the putter. It was not until 2008 that I discovered that the subconscious mind was the main participant to reinforcing the YIPS – but also a means to its elimination. It was then that Peaceful Golf was metamorphically formed, and the Peaceful Golf application was tested and refined over the next few years to help make a round of golf less draining and more enjoyable.

Peaceful Golf allows the mind and body to be rejuvenated while playing golf, not become exhausted. Are you tired after a round? If so – then you are probably playing *cognitive or awareness* golf. While this can be fun, more times than not a level of frustration from an off-hit or a missed easy putt could quickly ruin a fun time. Peaceful Golf allows the subconscious mind to do the habitual work while playing, and allow the cognitive mind to prepare, enjoy the moment and experience the beautiful surroundings. The fun part about the Peaceful Golf process is that it can be applied to other parts of your life.

Any element of your life you would like to change can be accomplished by using the same concepts learned; just replace the golfing stuff with the information related to the area to be changed. For example, if I wanted to quit biting my nails, I would replace the golf wording with growing healthier nails. Notice I did not convey that I would stop biting my nails – I will explain the reason for this in just a bit. First, I will briefly explain what led to the development of this inconspicuously effective concept

2 UNDERSTANDING THE SUBCONSCIOUS MIND

My professional experience as a mental health specialist was the spark to finding a solution to the YIPS and creating Peaceful Golf. I recognized that the YIPS is a behavior that is quietly learned and reinforced over time. However, since the behavior is learned, it can be "unlearned." This revelation was recognized while helping clients "unlearn" all types of unwanted behaviors. My research led me to the understanding that the subconscious plays an important role in everyday life, and especially with the belief system, so it must be a major part of what is learned when playing golf.

The sub-conscious mind is a fascinating facet of the thinking process. It is very child-like and weak, but it runs the show and is extremely resistant to change – just ask anyone that has tried to lose weight or stop smoking. The subconscious is similar to a computer program that never stops running. It collects every bit of information it receives through the senses, and stores the information. Every night the subconscious will eliminate unwanted material through the process of dreaming. This is the main reason why we have eclectic and bewildering dreams. However, any information that contains an emotional link or deemed important to the subconscious will be stored for the future.

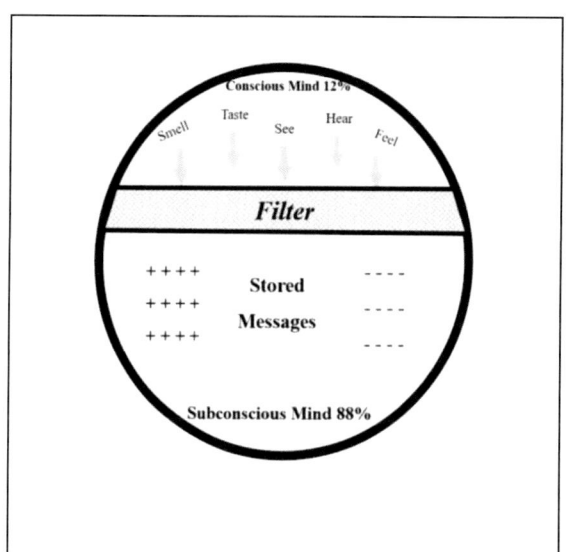

Look at the diagram. This concept of the mind contains three areas: conscious, filter, and the subconscious. Since I like to keep explanations simple, this is really all we need to know about the mind to have a grasp of why the subconscious is important to golf...especially Peaceful Golf. The conscious mind receives messages from the senses. It does not matter if the information being received is from tasting, hearing, visualizing, touching or smelling – the information is collected and analyzed, reasoned and decided upon with a logical conclusion. During the analyzation process, the information is delivered to the mind's filter. The filtering system immediately eliminates information that has been previously stored. Did you notice the comment about immediate elimination? This is in reference to similar information that is already stored in the subconscious – which is why changing an established behavior (example = smoking) is so difficult. If the information about the current incident has been previously established, then the information will be retrieved from the subconscious, which is where it is stored for future reference. This is why we react to certain situations the same way, like craving chocolate.

In regard to golf, if a 3-footer is needed for par, a golfer may have previously missed many of the tap-in putts– so the information of repeatedly missing the 3-footers has already been stored in the subconscious...and probably with an unpleasant emotional attachment. As the golfer steps up to the 3-footer, more than likely the thought of trying not to miss the 3-footer will be immediately retrieved from the subconscious. Since the message of missing the putt is already in the subconscious, and the subconscious really does not like negative words (i.e. not), which it simply ignores, then the message being delivered to the mind is, "I am trying to miss this 3-foot putt." Seems silly that a golfer would have such a thought, but this is what the subconscious is actually formulating.

Since the subconscious runs the show, the message is quickly delivered to the conscious mind and the muscles, and the desire to miss the putt is accomplished. It doesn't matter if it is a push, pull, jab, or ram – the goal of the subconscious is to satisfy the requested message – which is to miss the putt. Interestingly, this is the basis for the putting YIPS. Here is an example of how the subconscious operates. While playing golf with a friend in Boone, North Carolina (By the way, there are many lovely courses in the area.), since I had never played the course, my friend was trying to help me on each hole by explaining the best strategical approach and what to avoid. But, he was telling me that I should not hit it to an area of each fairway. My conscious mind had registered where not to hit the ball, but since the subconscious tends to ignore negative words, like the word "not" – the message circulating within the messaging system of my mind was, "Hit it to a particular area." My body reacted accordingly. I either hit it to the area I was warned to evade or I hit it completely to the opposite side due to my conscious mind trying to over-ride the unwanted message to hit to an unwanted area. The amazing part of this internal conversation is that it happens within a micro-fraction of a second without any conscious awareness.

Peaceful Golf works by simply allowing the incoming information to be translated into a positive message. Here is another example. During the 2006 U.S. Open, Phil Mickelson had a one stroke lead going into the final hole and upon finishing the hole his remark was, "…I can't believe I did that. I am such an idiot." Phil hit his tee shot to the left of the fairway, which was probably the only place he could have hit and remained in trouble. I have no proof, but there is a good chance the subconscious had received the message not to go left with the tee shot. Even if he got up to the 18th tee box and kept repeating to himself to keep it right, the message not to go left was already registered in his subconscious. Since the subconscious tends to ignore the word "not" habitually, the message to the body was "keep it left" – which is exactly what Phil did. The uniqueness of the subconscious is that it will naturally do whatever is needed to satisfy your messaged desires and work hard to guard you. It is a Divine built-in protective program. The footnote to Mickelson's mishap is linked to what happened after the tee shot. He has conveyed on television it was not the tee shot that got him in trouble, but the 2nd shot. However, if the tee shot had been in the fairway, the 2nd shot would probably not have been an issue.

In the iceberg illustration, notice how much larger the area is below the water's surface compared to the area above water. This iceberg illustration is a good analogy of the conscious and subconscious areas of the mind. The part above the water line is the conscious mind. The part below the water line is the subconscious. There is quite a difference. The conscious obtains about 12% of the mind, which leaves a whopping 88% for the subconscious. This simply means that a lot more is happening in the subconscious area - and there is much more room for storage. There is not a value placed on the information stored by the subconscious, nor does the subconscious know the difference between what is good or bad, heck – it cannot determine what is real and imagined. It is child-like, but like a child it will believe what it is told and is very resistant to change. Also, notice what is visible to the eyes if we were looking at the iceberg. However, what is visible is not in control.

So, let's revisit the 3-foot putt. If you continually tell yourself that you are lousy at making 3-foot putts, the subconscious is going to store the information. The thought is not evaluated as good or bad, but the next time you have a 3-foot putt - the conscious mind is going to register the challenge and in a fraction of a fraction of a second, the subconscious mind is going to recall the stored data about a 3-foot putt and send the information to the muscle-nerve connections to help you complete the thought you just had about the 3-foot putt, which is that you are lousy at 3-footers.

Here is something to consider. How many times have you nonchalantly rapped or backhanded a ball into the hole? Probably a lot. So why not putt like that all the time? Because when we start backhanding putts with the intention of making the putts – we place a conscious evaluation of when the backhands will start missing – especially if the putt has an attached value. When that miss eventually happens – the subconscious registers each of the missed nonchalant putts and the results eventually will become the same as the proper attempt – "I'm lousy at back-handing putts!" The key to the whole process is to remove the over-analytical thinking from the golfing process – which is what Peaceful Golf is all about.

The following is a wonderful example of controlling the analysis. Jack Nicklaus and Johnny Miller were playing an exhibition match in California. Johnny Miller had a putt of over 100 feet that had several steep breaks and numerous hills, with a downhill roll near the hole. An impossible putt by Miller's estimation. It was so impossible that Miller was hesitant to even attempt the putt. Nicklaus inquired about Miller's hesitation with a bit of sarcasm. Miller looked at Nicklaus bewildered. Nicklaus then asked Miller if he wanted him to show Miller how to putt it. Miller said, "Sure!" With the crowd laughing, Nicklaus approached the challenge with his usual confidence and threw down his ball next to Miller's ball, took a quick look at the terrain, stepped up to the ball and forcefully stroked the ball without a second of a thought. The ball traversed the hills and breaks and headed towards the hole at top speed. It hit the center of the back of the cup, jumped up and found the bottom of the cup. Nicklaus started to laugh, Miller was in disbelief, and the crowd was going wild. The important part of this scenario goes back to the approach that Nicklaus made prior to making the stroke, he limited the conscious thought. He let his inner thoughts control the stroke. Nicklaus, in my opinion, is one of the greatest pressure putters of all time, but if he had spent a lengthy time analyzing the putt, he probably would not have fared as well. Does this mean that analyzing a putt is not needed? Nope, but the concept of allowing the subconscious to do the work should be considered. By the way, a video of that fantastic putt can be viewed on YouTube.

Even though the subconscious runs the show and does not like change, change can take place. The key to any type of intentional change within the subconscious is to repeat the new (positive structured) message every day for a minimum of 24 days. Research has determined that it takes a little over three weeks for a new message, or desired behavior, to be kept within the subconscious. The best time to deliver the new message, or desired behavior, is right before you go to sleep. In fact, it is best to be sleeping while the new message is being presented to the subconscious mind. This should also be a hint that the message will need to be recorded and played in the evening – but, any time of the day will work.

Knowing that it takes 24 days to place a new positive thought within the subconscious, let us consider the example of first-tee jitters. If I had first-tee jitters and I wanted to design a thought for the subconscious so that my jitters would be less influential with my ball striking ability, I would design it with the same wording that would be used to communicate with a first-grade student, and be directly to the point. It would be something like this, "Okay, Dan. The first tee is the same as the 5th tee, grass, fairway, landing target. Your swing is the same and your confidence is the same. Smooth take away, let the club do the work, keep your eye on the ball, and swing the club with confidence." This is all that is needed to eliminate the first tee jitters. Really, it is! Notice that there is not a single negative word. There are no words that can be linked to the causes of first tee jitters, like " Man-oh-man, all those people are watching me. What if I whiff and make a fool of myself? Whatever you do, don't hit it into the trouble on the left. And don't dribble it to the ladies' tee, but - please don't whiff." That's a lot of thinking on the tee box, mainly due to other folks awaiting their turn to play - and watching you. Don't feel bad if this resembles you – the pros have the same experience – especially with the pressured events like the Ryder Cup matches.

3 CONSCIOUS CONFLICTS

The conscious part of golf is needed, but mostly during practice or learning. Conscious conflicts in golf are typically the thoughts that over analyze a swing, which includes identifying possible negative outcomes. These thoughts can occur days before actually playing a scheduled round. It is not uncommon to start analyzing the round, the swing, the wonderful outing…even the first tee shot. Interestingly, the thoughts do not have to be related to golf - it can be related to any subject. Let's go back to the first tee. It is amazing what can visit the mind while waiting to tee off. The list of topics can cover more areas than an Internet news "home page" - covering every conceivable topic – in a negative way. But it does not matter because only one topic should be levitating in the mind – the target of the golf shot. Peaceful Golf allows the mind to easily focus on the goal at the most appropriate time, without consciously forcing the process. During the 2017 ANA Championship on the LPGA tour, the television commentators talked about all the thoughts going through a player's mind when sizing up a difficult shot, but ultimately concluded that only one thought should be existing – the desired result. How does one get to the desired result without bringing in the negative possibilities? By training the mind. Training the mind to focus on positive outcomes with each option is the most efficient way – then, select the best course of action from the presented options. This will eliminate the negative attachments. Peaceful Golf allows the process to be instinctive, instead of analytical. How is the mind trained to make the process instinctive? By messaging the subconscious mind.

Conscious conflict is such a natural process, that it is rarely noticed. Typically, the mind is constantly bombarded with conflicting information. Because of the constant flow of information, it just becomes tired and simply selects the most convenient option to avoid further mental taxation. Take for example ordering fast-food at a drive-thru window. The thought of stopping and getting a quick meal and getting back on the road to the designated destination is comforting and gastronomically satisfying. However, when arriving to the ordering area, the ordering process tends to create muscle tension. "Is the speaker system going to work? Will the food preparers get the order correct? The menu has a lot of options; I wish I had time to review and choose! Dang, I dropped the money in the space beside the seat." What started as a simple task of ordering a quick meal, quickly transformed into a moment of tension. All the thoughts experienced at the drive-thru lane were previously stored in the subconscious mind – and most every time the drive-thru lane is selected, the same feelings and thoughts will be retrieved from the subconscious. This is the mind's natural reaction. This is done with everything that the mind and body experience. The only way to change the information in the subconscious is to continuously have positive experiences at a drive-thru. Unfortunately, the chance of this happening on a routine basis is very low. So, the reinforcing thought of what typically will transpire with a drive-thru is repeatedly experienced, which strengthens the negative impact, yet the drive-thru area is repeatedly visited in hopes the experience will be pleasant. With golf, the process is similar. Repeating thoughts will reinforce the action, especially if it is negative. Since humans find focusing on the negative easier than focusing on the positive – the negative is placed in the subconscious. Give some thought to this the next time you are trying to decide on how to play a hole. I enjoy par 3 holes that require a hit over water. I enjoy it because I always listen to my playing partners discuss what to do to avoid the water. Since they have already acknowledged the water as trouble, the chances of hitting the green are very slim. However, if all of the troubled areas are removed from the mind prior to hitting the ball, and the target of the green is the focus of attention – hitting the green is a high probability. Unfortunately, most golfers carry the trouble with them to the tee.

4 THE COMMON APPROACH TO CURING GOLF WOES

Byron Nelson enjoyed sharing the story of conveying to his wife that he needed a new driver because he was having a bit of trouble driving the ball consistently in the fairway. Unfortunately, his wife had not had a new dress in a long-time due to their financial restrictions during the early days of tour life. Yet Byron was convinced a new driver would help solve his driving woes. His wife, a bit agitated, made a sarcastic comment that conveyed that maybe it was not the driver, but the person driving the ball. This seemed to awaken Byron and brought home the truth – the cure is not always external.

Today's club technology is amazing. There are always tools to help a golfer hit straighter, putt better, concentrate deeper, and to never ever leave a ball in a bunker. Of course, these "cures" have been around for a long time, just not as advanced. Look at any early edition of a golf magazine and an advertisement can be found of how to obtain lower scores. The most common approach is to purchase something new. A new pair of shoes, a special fabric shirt, vitamins to enhance endurance, and shoes to maintain a healthy back. New items continue to be presented every year – just go to the annual PGA golf show in central Florida to see the latest and best items in golf. These various cures do work at times, but they are typically temporary, which is why there are so many new devices available yearly.

It is especially interesting that when a professional golfer wins with a unique putter, usually there are a slew of players that will gravitate to that style of putter. This happened on the PGA tour with the success of Dustin Johnson and his putter. After winning his first major tournament, fellow PGA players started using the same putter and LPGA players also started using it. It does not have to be a new club, just a different club will work. Take for example the putter Lee Trevino found in a house he was renting during the 1968 U.S. Open. He found an old putter, liked it, asked if he could use it – and he won the U.S. Open. There is a very popular picture of him giving the putter a gentle kiss.

The newness concept is the same thought that players are starting to use with gripping a putter. The grip change provides a temporary escape from the putting distress that a player may be experiencing. What I find especially intriguing is if professional golfers are struggling with putting consistently, then why should amateurs and weekend golfers be upset with the same issue? Don't the professionals practice daily? Do weekend golfers? Usually not, but they do expect professional results.

Changing a grip can be a great temporary fix, but eventually one will run out of grip options. During the 2017 ANA Championship on the LPGA tour, Michelle Wie used three different grips before stroking each putt. She started with a traditional grip, aligned her putt, switched to the claw-grip, focused on the putt to be attempted then changed her grip to a traditional grip with the right forefinger pointing straight down the shaft – and then within a second of shifting to the last grip style, she would stroke the ball. This worked quite well. Why? Simple. Before the mind could determine what she was about to do, she changed the grip, then putted the ball. It was temporary confusion. Mickelson has even incorporated a modified version of the quick grip-change. However, the mind quickly orients itself to the change due to a consistent pattern that is typically used on every green, and the unwanted behavior will simply reappear in the same form of which it previously created havoc. With putting, it is usually in the form of the YIPS.

So, how does a golfer keep the YIPS from taking over the putting stroke or the golfing mind? Since the YIPS are developed in the mind, the solution is in the mind. It should also be noted that since it took a long time (approximately 4 weeks) to develop the YIPS, it takes the same amount of time for the elimination. The best way to make a long term positive change is through the subconscious mind. Interestingly, the subconscious does not like change, so when a twitch is present during a crucial putt or one of those three footers that is easier to make with a back-handed slap stroke, the subconscious mind will simply repeat what it has been trained to do – stab at the putt, jerk the putt, become frozen, slice the putt, hit the putt fat – or anything other than the smooth simple stroke that was so easy to execute when first introduced to the game.

I experienced this many years ago at a putting exhibition. There were several celebrities present and a local television announcer. There were 50 – 60 folks surrounding the putting area, and I was nervous because of my YIPS. I made several attempts at a 20-foot putt and was close - but no success. The local television reporter was talking to the television audience and local observers about the challenges of putting, stepped up to the putt and made it on her first attempt. The crowd looked on with amazement and cheered the results, then looked at me for my remarks since I was the professional and did not make the putt. I was embarrassed with my attempts, but applauded the success of the reporter. Later that evening I reflected upon the moment and realized there was no pre-assumption on the reporter's part, just a nice stroke to place the ball on track to the hole. My thoughts were polluted with hopes of not making a fool of myself. The freeness of the reporter's mind should be the goal of every golf shot. To obtain the freeness, it is a necessity to train the mind to remain focused on the target – and training the mind to be free of mental pollution

5 COMPETITION

Regardless of the caliber of golf, competition is a natural experience, and hard to avoid. Whether competition is at the ultimate professional level, or as simple as executing a shot to make a par, it is a part of the game that creates the excitement of success. Bobby Jones tried to compensate for the personal competition by playing against "old man par" during his peak years, but he was still competing and feeling the pressure of competition. His intensity during a match was so high that it was not unusual for him to drop 10 – 15 pounds in one day. Over the course of his competitive career, this had to have taken a toll on his mind and body.

The interesting part about competition is that the duress of any competition is self-induced. Take for example the professional golfer that needs a par on the last hole to win a championship. The player has probably parred the hole many times, but the title and rewards associated with the title places an enormous amount of pressure on the professional golfer to succeed, but the hole has not changed. The design of the hole is the same. The strategy to play the hole has not changed. So, what now makes the hole 100 times more difficult? The value placed upon the hole or the event. The value is established from within the mind.

   Take, for example, a conversation between Gardner Dickinson and Arnold Palmer. During practice rounds, Gardner would beat Palmer on an even basis, so Dickinson asked Palmer why it was so that Palmer could win majors and he (Dickinson) could not. Palmer said the answer to that question was easy: Dickinson cared too much about winning a major. Palmer knew that he had what it took to win a major, so he placed less value on the event, and just played golf. When he did think of something other than playing golf, it typically cost him – like it did in the 1966 U.S. Open. This was the U.S. Open of which he held a comfortable seven stroke lead over Billy Casper with just nine holes remaining, yet, Palmer was also within reach of breaking Ben Hogan's record score for the U.S. Open. Palmer placed his mind on the record and not on just playing golf. The value he placed on breaking Ben Hogan's record was a misplaced value and it cost him a major championship. Here is an interesting aspect about the messages unknowingly being sent to the subconscious. When Palmer and Casper were standing on the tenth tee during the final round, Casper shared his thoughts with Palmer that he did not have a chance to beat him. Palmer, in a jokingly manner, conveyed to Casper not to worry about it – that he would do anything he could to help him – for Casper to just make some birdies and he would be fine. He did. The subconscious should not be underestimated of how much control it has over the conscious mind. Palmer expressed a thought that the subconscious acted upon - and he proceeded to bogey five out of nine holes and eventually lost to Casper. He did exactly what he said he was going to do; he did all he could to help Billy Casper.

   Competition causes the body and mind to react per the value placed upon the event. It is important to attain an understanding of how a self-determined value can influence the level of discomfort. Here is a personal example. In 1975, in my early 20s, I played in the final match of the World Putting Championship in Columbus, Ohio. First place was $50,000 – which was more than what any of the PGA/LPGA major tournaments awarded that year. Was I nervous? Absolutely. However, I also knew that if I kept focusing on how much I was playing for, I would continue to be nervous. So, to offset the nervousness, I thought about an amount of which I could play for with comfort. That amount was $10. I placed a value of $10 on the match and convinced myself that it was ok to play for $10 and just concentrate on each stroke, that it would be nice to win $10 and have a free dinner. It worked, because I was never nervous during the match – and my focus remained on each stroke of the match.

Let's consider another example utilizing one of the greatest, if not the greatest, golfer of all time – Jack Nicklaus. Nicklaus, the all-time major championship winner, was rarely nervous playing in a major championship due to the assessment he placed on each title. Did he have jitters? Sure, but he wasn't scared. Nicklaus knew of his golfing potential. The value he placed on each title never exceeded his ability, thus, his concentration and focus was at the appropriate intensity for each tournament. Although he always wanted to win, his focus was on the value of his performance, not the value of the results – that came later. If you review his performance in the majors, you probably will not find a situation where he had a title won, then lost it due to his playing. However, Nicklaus' body did react to the value he placed upon the majors. If you look at photos of him playing in the majors, you will see a consistent fever blister on one of his lips. This was his body's natural reaction to stress, which makes sense, since a fever blister is a virus that lies dormant in nerve cells until something causes it to become active, like stress. Interestingly, he consistently got fever blisters four times a year.

For the uniquely skilled golfers, competition is used to verify their ability. They strive to place themselves in the ultimate level of competition to test whether their skills and nerves will succumb to the test. The fascinating part of this process is that the success of the test is a rare accomplishment. By success, I mean meeting all expectations of the event. It is infrequent. Golfers know this, yet still strive to experience a slight sight of the successful moment. The rare accomplishment seems to eradicate the many moments of disappointment. To get to experience the success of golf, skills must be improved and the mental game must be solid. Concentration must be maintained throughout the event, and the self-induced pressure must be managed. Regardless of the level of competition, the requirement to handle the pressure to win is still the same. Peaceful Golf is an excellent tool to utilize to maintain concentration, regulate nervousness, and play with confidence. It allows the element of your game, that typically causes frustration and inhibits success, to be effortlessly managed. It is accomplished by utilizing the proper messages to the subconscious mind.

Competition is healthy. It provides the momentum to reach goals, the persistence to become better, the strength to concentrate, and the opportunity to experience rewards. However, competition can cause the body to react unfavorably. The body reacts to the messages provided to it by the mind. If the messages are linked directly to nervousness in specific situations, then the body will react to each similar situation in the same way. The repeated behavior becomes a habit for the mind/body reaction and is reinforced every time the reaction is repeated. Over time the familiarity of the repeated situation can provide enough comfort to successfully manage the uncomfortableness, but eventually the body returns to the nervous reaction without notification. The best way to eliminate the nervous reaction is to place a positive message in the subconscious to replace the nervous behavior. As always with subconscious messaging, the new message needs to be repeated a minimum of 24 days straight, and it is best to do it right before going to sleep.

6 UNDERSTANDING AND OVERCOMING THE YIPS

I was never aware of the YIPS or what the symptoms were to signify that the YIPS had taken residence within my mind. However, the first indicator was in an important match for the 1977 World Putting Championship. I was in a sudden death playoff, and I had a 12-foot putt for birdie. It didn't seem like much at the time – but I found it extremely difficult to pull the putter back, and when I did, my awareness of hitting the ball was removed. The very next vision I had was the view of a crippled ball hobbling towards the hole and stopping four feet short. I was stunned and bewildered. After making par, I watched my opponent make his birdie and smilingly shook my hand with an appreciation for winning the match. I didn't ponder the incident too long, but I would have the same experience some weeks later at another event, and then the YIPS became a regular visitor.

I researched the phenomenon, and learned that some famous golfers experienced the same sensation; however, an explanation of how to overcome the YIPS was missing from the literature. This started me on a lengthy research to find the means to control the unwanted actions. It is a phenomenon that is currently a bit more prevalent. I have watched PGA and LPGA players switch grips, putters, stances, swings, and superstitions in hopes of overcoming the mental vulnerability. I have anguished over amateurs missing 1-foot putts and angrily tossing their putters to instill punishment on the club for making the player look foolish. But, amateur golfers really should not be embarrassed or dismayed by having the YIPS. One of the greatest golfers of all time had the YIPS. The great Harry Vardon, 6-time British Open Champion, explained how he missed a 6-inch putt due to the jerking motion in his right hand while putting. It didn't happen every time, but it did happen enough times that it made Harry Vardon ponder if the right hand was going to twitch - which was a distractor from the most important part of putting – concentration. Some folks may not categorize Vardon's twitch as the YIPS, but all of the indications that Vardon provided sure makes it a YIP fit.

YIPS are an interesting phenomenon of golf. Although it is not restrictive to the game of golf, it is commonly associated with golf - especially putting. The YIPS do not suddenly appear; it is a gradual process of which negative messages are stored within the subconscious mind. A good analogy would be that the YIPS are as gradual as dust on a table. You don't really notice it, and then suddenly, the dust is covering the beautiful wood. If only wiping the mind, like wiping a table, could eliminate the YIPS. But, it can be just that easy.

The interesting part about the putting YIPS is that the more often short putts are missed, the more opportunities that negative messages linked to short putts are going to be reinforced in the subconscious. Here is an important element about this process. It takes approximately 24 days of a repeated action for a new behavior to become a habit (good or bad). This means the putting YIPS could invade all the golfers that play on a regular basis – especially if golfers place a high emotional value on putts. Fortunately, most folks have a few good putts in a round of golf to break the negative messaging being stored and reinforced; however, when placed in a situation of which the mind can recall a previous scenario that is similar to the current situation, then the body will react to the message the subconscious mind previously stored. In the case of a 3-foot putt, the body will either follow the subconscious message (i.e., "I always miss these!") or try to over-ride the message. For example, if a player consistently pulls 3-foot putts, and the message to the subconscious is that the short putts are never made due to constantly pulling the putt – then this is the message the body will receive the next time it is faced with a 3-foot putt. If putts are always missed by pulling the putt, the body may force a pushed putt. Or, as experienced with Ben Hogan, freeze over the ball.

Isn't it fascinating that a multi-major champion, a survivor of a deadly car crash, and a player that literally willed himself to a championship level of play – could be frozen by a 3ft putt? Hogan would stare at the ball for long periods of time - only because he was incapable of starting the backstroke. He was usually fine with lengthy putts, but if he were to get close to the hole and be forced to putt what would be considered a makeable putt – say three – four feet, he would experience the YIPS. Why? More than likely it was the conflict between the subconscious message and the physical reaction – which caused the muscles to freeze. Interestingly, trying to overcome the conflict with a physical domination is what creates the jab or jerking motion. The subconscious is just that powerful.

In regard to short putts, one of the main problems with short putts is thinking that an easily makeable putt should not be missed. Professionals miss them, so why should amateurs think they shouldn't? YIPS do not always involve a twitch or a yank: they can simply be negative thoughts that interrupt the golf swing or putting stroke. A player with the YIPS could start pondering what others are thinking. Internally the dialogue could be so berating of missing another short putt, anger is released upon missing. What about the snickering and laughing? It is certainly embarrassing and self-defeating. Players that stand frozen over a putt have related their internal conversations with me. It usually involves the following: "This is dumb, just hit the ball – who cares who laughs? Think about all the trouble in the world, and you are worried over a 3-foot putt – just hit it. I will look so foolish when I miss this." That is a lot of work for a 3-foot putt. If you have those conversations, you are not alone. I know that internal dialogue and those embarrassing feelings all too well. Before developing the Peaceful Golf concepts, when I played a round of golf with folks that knew of my putting accomplishments, and I would miss some short putts, some of the reactions were expected, yet hurtful. There would be a few laughs, some "I didn't expect that!" responses. But the most hurtful were the comments like, "C'mon Dan. That is not like you!" The pressure used to really build when I would play in team events. As mentioned earlier, I had the YIPS for many years and have read just about every book on the subject that is available...and tried various solutions. Nothing worked; so, I conducted my own research and discovered that some of the techniques I utilize as a mental health practitioner could also be used to help eliminate the negative messaging that develops the YIPS. If you have the YIPS, you will enjoy the next chapter, I will explain an effective approach to controlling and eliminating the YIPS.

7 ELIMINATING THE YIPS

There are a lot of books that present information about the YIPS, and even go as far as to explain what would be needed to control or eliminate the YIPS, but they really don't explain how the YIPS can be removed. Even though there has been a substantial amount of research that has been done about the YIPS, there is not a clear indicator of the cause; however, there is a unified agreement that it is a learned behavior. If the YIPS are learned, then the YIPS can be removed; however, based on my experience in mental health - a new behavior must be put in its place. The mind does not like a void. If something is going to be removed, it must be replaced. And remember, for a new thought to replace the old thought, it must be repeated for 24 days without interruption. If not, the previous thought will be retrieved. This is the basis of subconscious messaging. As most golfers know, the YIPS are most often associated with putting; however, it can be linked to any other facet of the golf game. I've seen lots of folks with the "Driving YIPS" or the "Pitching YIPS" – which causes the same severe embarrassment due to the many eyes watching an unsuccessful attempt to make a successful strike of the ball.

Professional golfer, Tommy Armour, is a good example. Armour was a combat veteran of WW I before becoming a professional golfer in 1924. He established his credentials as a skilled golfer rather early and just three years later won the 1927 U.S. Open. However, the real interest of this professional golfer happened just one week after the U.S. Open, at the Shawnee Open. Armour would establish history again by scoring the largest number of strokes on one hole, 23 strokes on a par 5. The history of the event is not recorded, but indicators convey that from the 17th tee, he hit 10 balls out of bounds. YIPS? Probably, mainly because Armour is credited with coining the phrase "YIPS" when he described his experience with the phenomenon.

Since the YIPS can be removed by using subconscious messaging, why aren't folks using it? I don't know. But I can convey a bit of bewilderment of not seeing anything about the approach in any literature I researched when I was struggling with the YIPS. However, I have used subconscious messaging very successfully and can now play at the highest level of competition without feeling the sensation of the YIPS or struggle to keep the thoughts of the YIPS confined. I have also helped many other professionals by using the same simple technique. I utilize subconscious messaging because it is the most efficient means to make long term changes to unfavorable behavior. There is not much effort required, and the subconscious will do its best to accommodate once it accepts the new message about the wanted behavior. For this to work the message needs to be presented to the subconscious for a minimum of how many days? Yes, 24 days, straight. If you skip a day – start over. Once the subconscious message is confirmed after the 24-day process, the information will be stored and will remain in the subconscious. For some folks, the time frame may be longer than 24 days, and for a special few – it can be shorter.

How are the messages being delivered to the subconscious?

By listening to an audio recording right before going to sleep. A sample recording for relaxation is available at my website store at **www.peacefulgolf.net.** This is a generalized relaxation recording, not a recording to help with the YIPS. It is simply to give you an idea of what a recording will sound like and its effectiveness. Regardless of the purpose of the recording, after the messaging has been established in the subconscious, I recommend listening to the recording on a regular basis, maybe once a week, merely for maintenance. If you are listening to a recording to eliminate the YIPS and happen to feel the sensation of the YIPS returning, just return to listening to the recording for a 24-day period. The positive messages will eventually over-ride the negative and the concern for the YIPS will become a distant thought…or not a thought at all.

Remember, it has taken a lengthy bit of time to develop the YIPS, so, it will take some time to eliminate the YIPS. I have included in this book specific guidelines of how you can create your own recording. Not to worry-- if you don't want to make your own recording, I will be happy to do it for you. Just go to the Peacefulgolf.net website and request a personal recording.

8 PEACEFUL GOLF

The golf swing is naturally challenging, but when the mental aspect of the game provides additional complications – the fun part of golf gets diverted. Just watch folks on a golf course and you will ponder why golfers continue to abuse themselves. Interestingly, when it all comes together for that one special drive, or chip-in or making a lengthy multi-breaking putt – it rejuvenates the desire to play more golf. When considering the two main elements of the game, the mental aspect and the skill aspect, which one is the most enjoyable to practice for improvement? I imagine most folks would select the physical skill level due to the immediate gratification and the tangible barometer. Just look at a driving range or a practice putting green – players of all skill levels are working diligently to improve their golfing proficiency.

A round of golf is unique in that if one part of the game is off a bit, another part of the game can take up the slack. For example, when the driver isn't working, the chipping may save the round. When the chipping is off, the mid-irons may come to the rescue. However, putting is a bit different. When the putter is un-cooperative – well, the game can be downright frustrating. This may be because a 2-foot putt is just as valuable as a 280-yard drive.

Golf can be infuriating, but learning and improving makes the game fun. The beguiling part about golf is that the mental game is just as important as the physical game. And just as with the physical part of the game, the mental aspect of the game can be offensively pernickety. One day the thoughts can be peacefully blank with a wonderful feel for each swing – the next day the thoughts can be cloudy with concerns about every detail of life – even that darn gnat won't stay off the ball.

Or what about the element of success? A 15-handicapper may have 4 pars in a row, but - when are the bogeys going to start? When the mental aspect of the game is not flowing and supportive, it really does not matter what the skill level is – the game simply loses some appeal. Regardless of what is causing the mental strife, learning to play golf at peace makes the game much more enjoyable, even at the highest level of competition.

When I reference Peaceful Golf, I am not talking about a universal harmonious status that religiously places you in the good tidings of your Higher-Power, but more of a frame of mind that allows golf to be played minus internal and external distractions. It is the comfort of addressing the ball without a thought pattern that dictates the next step in the procedure or trying to focus on an element of the swing during the actual swing or even contemplating a portion of the golf hole that should be avoided. Peaceful Golf is simply a free-flowing movement - with productive results. It is attainable by placidly embedding and maintaining progressive positive messages to the subconscious.

Let us consider a 15-handicapper. After numerous pars, a mid-handicapped player will probably start thinking about when the pars will end or trying to break 80 or focusing on protecting the round from being ruined. If water happens to come into play with the last few holes that could ruin the round, the thoughts could simply be, "Just don't hit it in the water, swing smooth and avoid the water." This seems like a solid thought for the shot, but what the subconscious mind is actually hearing is, "Hit it in the water, swing smooth, the water." Why does the subconscious mind hear the different message? Because the subconscious does not grasp the value of negative words. The subconscious purposely ignores the negative words and places emphasis on the remaining words. You may read the above subconscious-thought-sentence and think that it is not grammatically correct, but the thought only needs to make sense to a 6-year old because the subconscious mind communicates on the same level as a 6-year old – but, interestingly, the content of the message can be so strong that it dictates the results. For example, a child that is not getting his or her way does not know how to communicate the level of frustration being experienced, so a temper-tantrum becomes the result. When a temper-tantrum is exhibited in public, and at home, adults quickly respond to diffuse the tantrum and maintain peace. The child receives attention, gets his or her way, controls the situation, and remembers what was done to gain control. The subconscious uses the same tactic; however, the subconscious will do everything in its power to help you accommodate the intent of the message. So, when the subconscious receives the message that you want to hit the golf ball in the water, it will comply. Your swing may be smooth, but club contact may be with the turf first, and not the ball – resulting in a "fat" shot. A golfer could easily over-ride the "fat" shot by quickly adjusting the swing and hitting it thin – which would probably result in a water shot. Isn't this what your subconscious thought you wanted? It would be easy to over-ride the subconscious thought of hitting it in the water, but the physiological over-ride would probably be a slice or hook, now placing the ball in a possible unfavorable lie – but the water would be avoided. Ha! The subconscious was beaten. Yep, but the results are not as favorable as when the subconscious messages are constructively positive and linked to how you want to play golf. The subconscious cannot make you a "scratch" golfer over-night if you are a 15-handicapper – but it can eliminate the wasted shots due to mental distractions.

If the subconscious ignores negative words, why not use reverse psychology? Something like, "Do not hit it in the middle of the fairway!" This may work at first, but with this approach the subconscious has already been told the reason for using the negative words – which sends a different message to the subconscious – that you are really wanting to avoid the trouble on the hole. If you thought it – it was delivered to the subconscious.

The key to the process is to develop the messages to the subconscious that will allow the focus to remain on the positive aspect of the golfing round. For example, instead of contemplating trouble on a hole when hitting a tee shot, think only about the landing area – the target. When facing a 3-foot putt for par to break 80 or 70 or 60, think about swinging the putter smoothly. Instead of pondering about what folks are going to think if you dribble the ball off the 1st tee, think about letting the club do the work.

The subconscious messages should be designed to address the difficulties that typically ambush a round. As mentioned earlier, the best method is to place progressively positive messages in the subconscious by putting the positive thoughts on a recording and listening to them right before going to sleep. If you go to sleep before the tape finishes – even better. The messages are meant to be for the subconscious mind, not the conscious mind. The only time that the subconscious is receptive to messages is when the conscious mind is at rest, which is when we are asleep or the conscious mind is distracted, like day-dreaming. Fortunately, the subconscious has a built-in protector to identify unimportant information and removes unneeded material in the form of dreams, which is why most dreams are bazaar. This is done whenever we sleep or nap. It is also interesting that the majority of our dreams are not remembered. The dream that is usually remembered is typically the one just prior to awakening.

I presented this earlier in the book, but it is so important I am stating it again. When listening to self-help recordings, it is important to listen to it for a minimum of 24 days in a row. Why does it have to be

24 days? Because research has shown that on the average it takes 24 days of concurrent repetition for a new thought or new behavior to be solidly stored in the subconscious. Most folks that listen to tapes for 24 days always expect some whistles or bells to designate the wanted behavior taking over; it just does not happen that way. It may be months before the transition is noticed, and then it will be more of a passing thought of how differently you feel. For example, a golfer that listens to a recording to help control the putting YIPS will typically be awaiting the YIP sensations to appear - and at the beginning of the process they may. However, the YIP sensations will unhurriedly be controlled and replaced by the newer thoughts and beliefs. Eventually the messages being sent to the conscious mind during stressful situations, like a 3-foot putt, will instead be directly linked to the target, a smooth stroke, and calmness. Will every 3-foot putt be made? Probably not, but the anxiety associated with the putt won't be the cause of the miss, and the barrage of insults that typically follow such a mishap will be avoided, thus allowing a more peaceful experience with the golfing outing.

9 HOW TO MAKE YOUR RECORDING FOR SUBCONSCIOUS MESSAGING

So, what about the recording? Some folks would like to make this a scientific process with technical guidelines. It is simply a conversation to yourself in 3rd person. There are a few elements within the sentence structure that should be avoided, not to worry, this will be discussed in a bit. But, the recording should be of your natural voice -- avoid the weird or spooky voice. The content should be stated in a positive manner, which is simply avoiding negative words. For example, if there is a hole that continually provides problems due to the trouble on the left – instead of conveying to the mind to not hit it to the left or avoid the left – consider using, "The right-center of the fairway is the target." Or focus on a more precise target, like "I'm fading the ball, so, the stake in the center of the fairway is the target." This places the mind's attention on a specific target and not on the troubled area.

The reason for practicing this style of wording is because the subconscious, as you now know, tends to ignore negative words. So, if not hitting it to the left is your thought before teeing off, the subconscious is going to receive an altered message due to not liking negative words. The subconscious will receive, "Hit it towards the left." When the focus is not on the positive or a specific target, here is what typically happens. The internal fight to avoid the left will become part of your mental conversation as you set up to hit the tee shot. The subconscious will repeatedly message the conscious mind and muscles to hit the ball to the left. Your natural rationalization will be to avoid the left. Most times than not, the subconscious mind, which communicates via imagination, will over-rule any other incoming thought; however, when the physiological action prevails – the result is usually an offline hit to the opposite direction – in this situation it would be a flared shot to the right...which would be avoiding the trouble on the left.

Here is a good way to envision the subconscious. Imagine the subconscious mind as an elephant. The conscious mind is you riding the elephant. You are in control, until the elephant decides to over-rule you. Once the elephant decides to go a certain direction, there is no way you are going to control it with your commands. That elephant is going where it wants to go regardless of the many commands you may yell at it. Interestingly, the subconscious is the same way. It will only act to accommodate personal needs, but the way the need is expressed is the important part of this process.

Communicating with the subconscious is not very difficult. To communicate with the subconscious productively: keep the wording on the level of a 6-year old, use positive wording, and provide the message in 15-20 minute segments. There is no need to compile a lengthy recording with every aspect of your golf game that needs adjusting. Select one area and start practicing the process. If you have more than one area, after 24 days, make a new recording – but link the prior concern with the new recording to allow it to be a reinforcing message.

Remember, a recording must be listened to for a minimum of 24 days without interruption for the new behavior to be accepted by the subconscious. When making progressive recordings, which are recordings that build upon one another, it is best to connect the sequel recording with a small bit of the previous recording to verify the connection, then introduce the new goal. For example, if the original recording goal was based on controlling first tee jitters, then the recording for this concern would be based on the objective to remain calm, focus on the ball, let the club do the work, and accept the results. If the second concern is being comfortable with short putts, the messaging for this concern would be linked to the first tee jitters. It would be similar to the following, "The tee shot is a fun way to start the hole, breathe calmly, and enjoy the day. Every time you tee the ball, you will find a sense of calmness and confidence as you prepare to play the hole. Take the fun to the putting green and make a smooth stroke to finish the hole. Remember to stick with your pre-shot routine and let the club do the work. Putting is fun, and you will provide the proper speed and make a smooth stroke every time you putt." If you start thinking about missing a two-foot putt and being embarrassed, then the next area of recordings should include something about having fun with short putts or remaining focused when putting short putts.

 It is even okay to tell the self to miss the putt smoothly. This form of reverse psychology eliminates the pressure of having to make the putt to avoid ridicule, and places emphasis on a smooth putt. The rationalization for this approach is that the mind becomes overloaded with unwanted thoughts when folks are watching and expecting the short putt to be made, which intensifies the embarrassment. By messaging to the subconscious that it is okay for the putt to be missed, the linking message derived from the subconscious will not be the same one that is usually retrieved to having to make the putt to avoid ridicule. Instead, the thinking of a missed putt places a bit of relaxation on the muscles. With the addition of stroking the putt smoothly, the chances of making the short putt will increase considerably since most missed short putts are the results of a quick jab, a jerk, or opening/closing of the putter head to avoid the anticipated embarrassment.

10 WHAT SHOULD BE CONTAINED IN THE RECORDING?

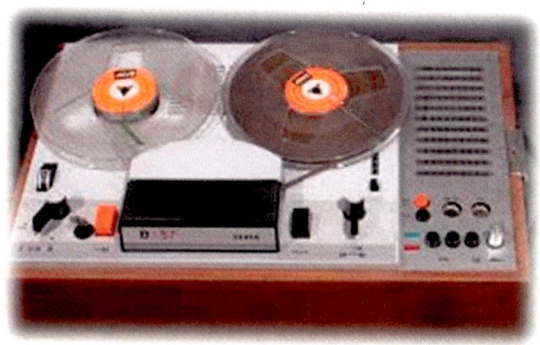

When a personal recording is considered, most folks twinge and start complaining about the sound of his or her voice. However, the subconscious could care less about the sound of the voice, it is only seeking beneficial information to be stored. If it is not going to be for the betterment of the self, the subconscious will remove the information before it is considered a stored option. So, eliminate the voice repulsion and focus on the content. If you don't want to record your voice, select a person whose voice you like and have him or her make the recording based on the script you provide. If you don't want to make a recording, I will be happy to do it for you.

As mentioned earlier, the content of the recording should be in 3rd person. Even if you know it is your voice, address yourself as an outsider. For example, when I create recordings for me, I always use my name. Here is an example of my introduction. "Okay, Dan, let's get started. I want you to place yourself in a relaxing position. Remember to avoid crossing your arms and legs..." If you prefer the first person, try it and see how it works for you, but I have found the best results to be with an outsider approach.

It would also be favorable to write your content before recording.

Read it a few times and then read it for the recording session. Remember, the subconscious is not seeking a theatrical read, so if you have a monotone voice – that is perfectly fine.

The length of the recording will depend on what is being accomplished. For example, a recording for managing weight can be as simple as, "From this point forward, Dan, the decision to eat healthier will be your focus. The portions you select will be the best size to help you attain a healthy body. The desire to consume more water will be continuous and a healthier choice over any other beverage. Have fun becoming heathier and preparing for a new and fitter look." Yep, that's it. By listening to those few words for 24 days you will start to make healthier choices. That is how powerful the subconscious mind is and how it will continually work for your betterment.

Now that you know what to include, what should be avoided? There are certain elements to avoid when making a personal recording. It is best to utilize positive words and avoid adverse words to construct your message. For example, read the following statement, "Now, Dan, I want you to stop smoking after every meal." Now, read the same statement and do not include the word "stop" within the reading. Even though the second reading may be grammatically incorrect, the message the subconscious will receive is literally conveying to smoke more, this is why the message should be in a positive frame. So, my alternative statement for the above situation would be, "So, Dan, after each meal every time you have the urge to smoke, the urge will be satisfied by drinking water." Another approach could be, "So, Dan, as you finish each meal that is contributing towards a healthier life style, continue the desire to be healthy by participating in activities that relate to healthiness. This could include drinking more water, or enjoying a fruit cup, or sipping some green tea or even taking a stroll. You have the power to make the healthiest decisions for your needs at each moment – enjoy the control and a healthier body." The latter statement provides a few options, with some encouraging thoughts. It does not need to be long and complicated.

It is best to maintain simplicity since the subconscious mind retrieves information the easiest when worded so that a 6-year old will understand it – but remember not to talk as if you are conversing with a 6-year old, which brings me to restating the next consideration - utilize your normal voice. Some folks try to use a mind-spelling voice or a lower-deep voice or dragging out certain words to attach a subliminal message to the content – but this is not necessary. Just read your message slowly and utilize your normal voice.

With the computer software that is available, it is easy to include a favorite tune in the background – but you may want to avoid the tunes with catchy lyrics, your mind may focus on the lyrics more than the improvement message. It is best to go with slow, soft instrumentals that do not have any association with lyrics. One that I like is, "On Golden Pond." It has a relaxing and comforting sound. I can easily visualize the late autumn sun glistening off the water and providing warmth to my face. The image is already in my mind from watching the movie, so the feelings are easily recalled as well. When including music to the background, be sure the volume is just high enough so it can barely be heard. The music should complement your voice, not be a distraction.

11 USING PEACEFUL GOLF CONCEPTS WITH EVERYDAY LIFE

The concepts of Peaceful Golf are not limited to golf. The means of attaining a peaceful life can be accomplished by using the concepts from the Peaceful Golf program - it just requires a bit of adjusting to reflect the areas of your personal changes. For example, public speaking seems to be a high anxiety event for most folks, but the anxiety is self-induced. Most folks worry about many factors other than the speech content while giving a speech, thus - the actual speech becomes overly challenging and produces a lot of anxiety. The most common distracting thoughts are related to grammatical mistakes, forgotten lines, and others' thoughts. The concept of Peaceful Golf can help a person remain at ease while standing in front of hundreds and deliver a successful presentation by messaging the subconscious to remain focused on the speech content and becoming comfortable with being in front of any size group. Most folks make life difficult by the reaction to events. Peaceful Golf can help manage the challenges.

12 JUNIOR GOLF

Golf provides a wonderful environment for kids to learn valuable lessons to prepare them for the challenges that life seems to naturally provide. For most, golf is play and a form of recreation; however, the competitive atmosphere is now provided for all ages. There are organized tours for youngsters that provide data that would impress PGA and LPGA statisticians. Because kids are learning to be competitive at an early age, it is important to also develop the mind to be competitive – but remain balanced.

Along with developing competitive skills, golf provides an opportunity for kids to experience self- improvement with immediate feedback. However, it is important to remember that the maturation process in golf is no different than life's maturation. It is slow, it is demanding, it is difficult, and it can be cruel. So, it is imperative for children to maintain a positive frame of mind and create a mental forcefield to combat negative thoughts. It is natural for parents to want to protect their children from negative experiences, and one of the best ways to do this is to build a positive inner belief so that negative experiences are simply accepted as an event – an event without a personal tag or label. Kids are easily influenced by the words of adults, and other kids. Just consider how easily influenced adults are by words that conflict with their personal beliefs – the same result happens with kids, but with a deeper deposit.

Kids naturally criticize themselves when they do not easily master a skill. They have learned this process. So, it is important to help kids to understand that golfing skills will take time to master and to become a bit more patient. Take chipping as an example. Chipping has so many variants involved with weight distribution, club angle, opening the clubface, and swing angles – that it is very challenging to master the skill. However, most professionals will convey that shots around the green are the score-savers in a round. Since the chipping skill is so challenging, kids become frustrated when the mastering of the various chipping techniques are not readily mastered. They may start to give up and allow the negative thoughts to enter the mind that chipping is too hard to learn and no fun. This can easily be avoided by placing emphasis on how much fun it is to learn the various aspects of chipping and becoming patient with the mastering of the skill. The message to the subconscious of being patient and wanting to learn the skills of chipping will over-ride the pouting response of not easily mastering the skill, thus setting up the ability to be patient with the learning process.

The Peaceful Golf method allows a child to construct an inner belief system to help ward off sabotaging thoughts that can become taxing and self-defeating. Also, knowing that kids are naturally resistant to listening and learning from parents, presenting the information while they sleep is a less stressful way to accomplish the task.

There are many programs to help junior golfers develop, so what is unique about Peaceful Golf? Diversity. Most programs have a pre-determined message for the participant. The starting point is where the program determines it should start, then the development is either based on satisfying a criteria or objectives - or the information is similar to motivational comments – temporary. Peaceful Golf takes a junior golfer's natural gifts and allows the development to be individualized. The areas of development and the time frame required will be determined by each junior golfer's personality and needs, and can be adjusted. There is no limit to what can be addressed or improved, and the results are long lasting. It is a perfect supplement to any existing training program.

13 SCRIPTS

The following scripts can be read into a recorder just as they are or you can personalize it with your name or situation. These scripts can be used for various areas within the game of golf; however, the words can be adjusted to accommodate specific areas within your game. If you are not pleased with your recording results, go to Peacefulgolf.net and request a personal recording. I wish you the best with the development of your golf game and reaching the ultimate level of playing golf peacefully.

1. First Tee Jitters

The first tee is a natural way to begin a round of golf. Upon stepping onto the tee area there will be a calm about you with the knowing that this is the way to begin a fun round of golf. As you tee the ball your focus will be on the target of the initial shot. The target awaits the landing of the ball, just let the club do the work. Keeping your eye on the ball and the target within your mind will be the initial step to having fun. Notice how calm and relaxed your hands are as they gently grip the club, and – the more people that are waiting to tee off, the more relaxed you become. Simply enjoying golf is what your day is about, so start off the round with a smile, relaxed and focusing on the target. And this you will also find to be true, every time you look at the ball when preparing to hit the next shot, the more relaxed and the more confident you will become, that's right, and your golfing day will be enjoyed. Be at peace with the day -- golf is fun.

2. Short Putts

Putting is a fun part of the game. All putts are makeable and the closer to the hole the ball is the more relaxed you will become – besides, you are closer to the hole than when you started. Each time you mark your ball and replace it to start your putting routine, you will find a wonderful state of relaxation and focus being present. The focus is on the target. Short putts are fun, and you will enjoy the opportunity to make each putt with a smooth and dedicated stroke. The results will be accepted with an appreciation for making a valid attempt. Remember, each time you get to putt it is a reminder of how much you enjoy playing the game of golf and knowing that each putt is a representation of your calm and relaxed demeanor when putting. This you will also find to be true: respecting the game, course, and your ability will provide the opportunity for you to play golf with a dedicated and peaceful approach.

3. Hitting over Water

While playing a round of golf there may be a shot that requires a hit over water. This type of shot is just as easy as hitting over turf. The ball is the same, the grip is the same, your swing will be the same – dedicated and fluid. Each time you hit over water and every time you look at the ball you will notice a calming confidence within your ability. This you will also find to be true, as you look at the intended target, the image of the water will provide calmness. Enjoy the day and the refreshing environment as you play golf. As you do, your focus will remain on the target as you make a fluid swing to send the ball to the intended target.

4. Increase Concentration

As you play golf, enjoy the day and the environment and the opportunity to test your skills. Each time you address the ball, tee the ball, look at a golf ball and address your shot – your focus will become sharper and determined. All other thoughts will be replaced by the intended target, and your swing will be dedicated to hitting to the target. This you will also find to be true: every time you start to feel anxious or nervous, you will notice your mind becoming dedicated to the target and an assuredness of playing to your best will fill your mind. The calmness demonstrated by your favorite professional under the most stressful condition will be replicated by you. The more the calmness is replicated, the more confident you will become with your ability. Regardless of the pressure of the situation or any uncomfortableness, the moment this is experienced, your focus and concentration will be directed to the target of the shot, and your instinct for each shot will enhance your natural skills. And any nervousness and anxiety will be the trigger to become calm and confident.

14 CLOSING COMMENTS

Peaceful Golf is designed for you to adjust the messages to the subconscious to make changes to your golf game to make golf more enjoyable. The application is limited only by your imagination. The overall improvement of your golf skills can be addressed or any individual part of your game can be improved. The mental game can be adjusted to eliminate negative thinking, and the fearful YIPS can be removed. The key to the process is to place your messages to the subconscious in a positive frame, record the message, and listen to it right before bed for 24 days in a row. You will then start to notice a slight encouraging difference with your game, but not really know why.

It is fascinating and amusing how the changes gently takes place. You don't even have to believe there is a subconscious mind to receive the benefits, the subconscious does not care. It is similar to understanding gravity. You know it exists because the concept was explained, but you don't really know why it exists, but things do fall, as with Newton's apple, so it must be present. Even if you don't believe in the concept of gravity, it is still working. Thus, the subconscious is always working and collecting information delivered from the senses. This may not seem important at first thought, but think about the information being delivered by way of television, movies, music, and conversation. If there is a song that is being played all of the time in your home, then your children, and you, will be receiving the message and the information will be stored in the subconscious if the music is being listened to on a daily basis. If you listen to the daily news, and the news is always negative in content, then your approach to life will probably be negative as well. The subconscious does not know if the information is good or bad -- it just stores the information so that it can be utilized if a scenario occurs that relates to the information stored.

There is a popular saying, "You are what you think" – and it is true. However, this can easily be a positive thought, and not negative; yet, since we naturally lean towards negative thinking – the negative messages are routinely stored – which may be why we are seeking to avoid trouble on a golf hole.

Since the subconscious is always working for you, you might as well tell it how to work. I have used subconscious counseling to help folks feel more relaxed, increase concentration, manage their weight, improve their golfing experience, and even expand their imagination. It is truly the easiest way to help you attain long term changes to immediate concerns, you will enjoy the process...and especially the results.

Peaceful Golf

Dr. Anders has worked in the mental health field for over 25 years and utilized subconscious counseling in his private practice. His doctorate degree is in behavioral science, with an emphasis in performance enhancement. He is an accomplished mental health practitioner and professional athlete. Dr. Anders believes that the subconscious mind is the driving force behind decisions and behavior. He has transferred that concept into a simple way to manage a golf game and overcome negative golf mentality - as well as eliminating the YIPS. He is available for Peaceful Golf presentations and workshops.

Made in the USA
Lexington, KY
24 April 2018